WHEN THE MIRROR SHATTERS

WHEN THE MIRROR SHATTERS

Breaking the Bondage of Performance Mentality

JENNIFER "KAYLENE" CARTER

CONTENTS

INTRODUCTION

THERE'S a crisis taking place in the entertainment industry right now. You don't have to look far to see examples of artists who seemingly had it all, yet felt empty inside and made self-destructive decisions. While some have succumbed to addiction or sought treatment for mental health issues, some have even committed suicide in a moment of desperation. If you woke up today, there is still hope. God can turn your situation around.

This is just one story: my story. I have twenty-five years of experience in the entertainment business, working in many different areas from artist to teaching the subject at college level. I've spent time with Grammy winners, record label executives, and movie stars. No matter what level you are at, there are opportunities to make positive decisions that can affect your path and bring you to a healthier place. That starts with how you see yourself. Take a look with me . . .

CHAPTER ONE

YOUR DAUGHTER IS SO PRETTY

Smiling for the Crowd, Crying on the Inside

As far back as I can remember, my biological mother had a bad habit of entering me into beauty pageants. In my baby keepsake book, there is a receipt for a photo contest she entered me in as an infant. I have several pictures of me as a baby in staged photo shoots, including one with me sitting in the middle of a row of dolls. That should have been a clue of things to come. The thing about the image that haunts me is that I was portrayed as a living doll (akin to a toy that you can set on the shelf when you are done playing with her). It was not the last time she treated me more like a possession than a human being.

When I was just a toddler, I lost a pageant after crying on stage because I couldn't have one of the balloons that was being used as a decoration. I would ask her later in life, "Why didn't anyone just give me the balloon and let me walk with it?" Unfortunately, the pattern of disregard for my feelings was set.

"Mother, You're Hurting Me"

ONE of my first memories from childhood was of me sitting in a frilly, hot pink dress in our bathroom at about four years old. My mom was brushing my hair furiously to prepare me for a pageant in a Florida small town. I distinctly remember the tense tone of my voice, saying, "Mother . . . you're hurting me."

She continued impatiently ripping away at my hair, unconcerned with my feelings. Aside from a mysterious scar on my stomach (and a disclosure later in life from a babysitter that had witnessed my mother abusing me at age two), things seemed okay for a few years. She was busy with college and working long hours (leaving me with numerous babysitters, coworkers, or neighbors). One such neighbor took a particular liking to me and encouraged me to call her "Mamaw," just as her biological grandchildren did. Some of my best memories took place with her, up until we had to move an hour away for my mother's new job.

Out of sight and accountability, my mother's temper turned dark. She seemed to change after my father married my newest stepmother and she started taking her anger out on me when I was only eight years old. She would often snap at me when I made a facial expression that she said reminded her of my dad. Then the beatings started.

I was left home alone after school as young as nine, but threatened that if I walked down the street to a classmate's house, there would be "consequences." She didn't want the neighbors to know, so she warned me that she would be calling at random times to make sure I was there. The overarching threat was that I would be punished if I didn't answer the phone. Even though I was always welcome at my childhood friend's house, I had no choice but to comply for fear of more physical violence. To combat the loneliness and escape my volatile home environment, I withdrew to my room with a radio where I discovered female vocalists new to the music industry. There was a trend in pop and adult contemporary music at the time where singers were showcasing their vocal ranges with stunning ballads. Their technique and skill captivated me.

Fascinated, I got their tapes from the local mall and started practicing every note over and over again until I could hit them all. Reading had always been a hobby since I learned to read at age three, but memorizing song lyrics and adding my voice brought the written word to life for me. I soon joined the chorus at my elementary school where I excelled, unbeknownst to my mother. She was wrapped up with charismatic church services that she had thrown herself into, starting when I was ten years old.

The services were run by a "faith healer" who had been known for tent revivals. His sons played music before each meeting. My mom seemed eager to "set me up" with one of the brothers. I had never had a boyfriend, since I was only in fourth grade. After initially agreeing to meet them, I grew tired and eventually crawled under the pew to fall asleep (the meetings would often last from 7pm until two or three in the morning). Undeterred in her new mission, my mom started driving us all over the state to see the family perform and minister.

When I Started Winning, I Started Losing Myself

A couple years (and countless church meetings) later, my mom took me to a bluegrass festival where the evangelist's sons were competing. After pressuring me to enter a beauty pageant that was also happening at the festival, I succumbed (though mostly from boredom). I would be stuck at this music event for days, alternating between assignments of running the boys' tape table or carrying instruments to babysitting their younger siblings while they were on stage. My mom bought me a blue dress with sequins, a large bow, and puffy sleeves.

To my shock, I won the pageant and even got to walk onstage for the festival audience afterwards. It was the first time I had gotten attention in the boys' world and they seemed somewhat surprised that the focus was on me. Shrugging it off as them seeing me as a little sister type instead of a beauty queen, I just smiled and basked in my temporary win. As the weekend wore on, though, it became apparent that one of the brothers (who was thirteen at the time, a year older than me) was apparently seeing me as more than a sister figure. After yet another session of selling their merchandise, he asked me to marry him. Taken off guard, I just laughed coyly and responded, "Where's my ring?"

I was on cloud nine for a while but, when we got back home from the festivities, I was quickly brought down to earth. On a weekend soon after, my mother started demanding that I pack my hot curlers and get ready to go to the mall. Annoyed that another Saturday would be wasted on a dog and pony show of sorts, I refused. She was visibly angry and stormed around the house, ignoring me and grabbing all my things. Seeing that she had made up her mind (and relieved that another disagreement hadn't turned into her physically abusing me again), I resigned myself to the front seat of our car and went through with the pageant.

My mom got me ready for the pageant in the restroom at the mall. I went through the routine of the forced smile and slow paced walk for the judges. To my surprise, I won . . . again. Instead of just an annual local pageant, though, this one was a stepping stone leading up to a national pageant which was to be held in Orlando, Florida. One of the judges approached my mother and gave her the information.

"Your daughter is so pretty," she began. I watched as another stranger gave me compliments, but it was my mother's face that lit up. "You get it from me," she would brag later. The only positive affirmations I ever got from my mom, in fact, were related to my looks or my intelligence (which was also hereditary, in her opinion). It seemed it had to be something that could be traced back to her because she wasn't interested in my unique personality.

What took place next was a whirlwind of shopping for multiple outfits, since the national pageant had many different categories each contestant could enter. There was sportswear, talent, and (ultimately) the formal wear competition. This pageant felt particularly awkward since I was shocked at the way the young girls dressed. I was in the preteen (10-12) division, yet the girls were dressed in backless, skintight, leather getups with heavy makeup on and hair shellacked with styling product.

Ashamed, I realized that I didn't fit in (as my clothes were normal for a child my age). I did place in the sports-wear competition, at least, dressed in an age appropriate shorts set patterned with sunflowers (though only at 4th runner up). For formal wear, I wore a huge white ball gown that looked more like a wedding dress to me, but was a stark contrast to my tanned skin (so at least I stood out). It wasn't enough to beat these girls who carried themselves like they were in their late twenties, some even wearing plastic caps to cover gaps where they had recently lost their baby teeth.

The most exciting thing about the pageant, to me, was getting to meet one of the judges afterwards. Being a latchkey kid, I had watched a lot of television to pass the time at home alone and this judge happened to be a host from a network that catered to children. This was the closest I'd come to meeting anyone "famous." To my surprise, he signed my contestant number (which I'd had clipped on my outfit until the pageant was over) with the words, "See ya on TV." He must have seen something in me that I didn't yet because his words would soon come true. . . .

This was a photo shoot that was staged
so I would look like a living doll. I always find
this ironic since my mother treated me like
a possession instead of a person.

This is the hot pink dress I remember wearing to a pageant when I was four years old.

This was another pageant, which took place in my hometown.

Here's my return to the pageant circuit
where I won first place.

CHAPTER TWO

IN THE SPOTLIGHT, UNDER A MICROSCOPE

"See Ya on TV"

THE female judge from the pageant at the shopping mall had also returned to judge nationals. She spoke to my mother after my subsequent loss and asked if she wanted to put me in local t.v. commercials in Orlando. Although she was acting as an agent, many of the gigs she got me were unpaid. She called it "good exposure." Soon, I was traveling as far as Jacksonville to shoot at different locations.

Commercials led to an appearance on a local television show that aired on a network in Orlando, which centered around a theme park. I did backup dancing and got to wear horror makeup, as it was a Halloween themed episode. My "agent" soon talked my mother into spending money as an "investor" for a t.v. pilot that was going to be pitched to national networks. I went through the audition process and read for the part with a now famous actress from Orlando. We both landed the gig. I joined a cast of nine other hosts including some who went on to sign pop music recording deals, perform on world tours, and appear on Emmy award winning t.v. shows.

Rising Stars

AT the time, none of us knew what the future held and when we finally got a $100 paycheck for a long day of filming, we were thrilled to be "professional" actors. We had access to backstage areas and front rows at concerts, as well as to backlots at theme parks that were currently filming popular shows. We interviewed pop music groups that were trying to launch their careers in America (after being promoted in the UK). I even got to be on set as one of these groups filmed the music video for their first single, which quickly became a hit song and made them celebrities.

I bought the single and was excited to share the story with my childhood sweetheart, who was home during the winter from his own performing schedule with his family. He was not impressed and made jealous comments about the singers in the boy band. I was crestfallen, but this behavior continued. During another interaction, he ripped down a headshot of my male co-host which I had in my room with all the posters and other memorabilia related to my budding acting career. Despite his jealousy, he had still not gone public with our romance or made clear his intentions for our future.

After finishing up the location shoots, the cast and crew all gathered together to film the main pilot on our very own set that the producers had built for us. My mom once again took me shopping for various outfits and I settled on a blue shirt that she had bought me the night before because it matched my cohost's choice of shirt. Flying off the handle out of nowhere, my mother started screaming at me on set because she thought the shirt made me look like a "boy." I was puzzled because blue was my favorite color, she had no problem with it when we were at the store less than 24 hours earlier, and (with stage makeup on and long hair to my waist, due to our religious denomination) I had never been one to appear masculine.

I was also humiliated because so many people witnessed the scene. Realizing her stage mom tendencies had reached a peak that was not manageable anymore, I decided to quit the entertainment industry. I would not return for two years. By then, most of my new friends would be scattered—some for promotional tours, one for a role on a soap opera in Los Angeles, one modeling in New York City, etc.

Finally Free

AFTER taking a break from the entertainment industry, I had plenty to keep me busy. I had to work extra hard during my sophomore and junior year to play catch up, as I had been homeschooled at a day school during my freshman year. This "school" was actually a halfway house for wayward girls (which my Mamaw balked at), but there were a handful of students that just came there to learn and left. My mother would sometimes threaten to have me committed to the house permanently for such "crimes" as sleeping past my alarm in the morning. This seemed to give her a sense of control since she could no longer beat me up, as my Mamaw had stepped in when I was thirteen and threatened to report her to the state.

The plan was for me to graduate high school in two years, but my teacher took advantage of the fact that I was done with my work quickly and would ask me to help her grade other students' work (which I did, to help pass the time until the next assignment). She then refused to grade *my* work (apparently not wanting to lose her free help). As a result, I was being held back from skipping a grade.

With my mother not able to ship me off to her "church" run seminary in Virginia (where my childhood sweetheart had his primary residence) at sixteen, her plan was coming apart. Instead, I returned to public high school with my friends and took advanced classes (plus summer classes) to get back on track, as none of my work during ninth grade transferred from the unaccredited day school.

My mother was now using verbal abuse and psychological games to hurt me, cutting me off financially during sophomore year, so I had to get a part-time job to pay for any school-related expenses (i.e. yearbooks, sporting event tickets, uniforms). I was about to get my drivers license, so my mom bought a car, seeming thrilled that the radio station was there doing a promotion. She had them announce the purchase over the county-wide radio station. Despite her using me for another "fifteen minutes of fame," the car wasn't put in my name. Instead, she used it as a constant way to manipulate me.

Nevertheless, my part-time job had opened doors to meet other friends who had cars and I was able to develop a social life of my own (outside of my mother's strict, religious circle). She didn't like my growing sense of freedom and, two weeks after my 18th birthday, assaulted me to seemingly beat me back into submission. She took it way too far, though, as she punched me around ten times on the left side of my head—violently shaking my head by my hair in between punches. Since she was driving down our street and I was in the passenger seat, I didn't feel I could defend myself or she might wreck the car.

In shock, after the car pulled into our driveway, I ran inside and called my best friend. I immediately packed a bag and fled to her house where I stayed for the first semester of my senior year. Soon after running away from home, I found a new job as a waitress where I tripled what I was making in retail and was finally able to pay my own bills.

Even after running away from home, I had managed to complete high school a semester early, so the principal allowed me to leave school. With my academic scholarship being processed, I was finally able to move away from my hometown. Though I couldn't afford a letterman's jacket or senior pictures, I put it behind me and looked forward to returning to my career in entertainment.

"Transcending" the Pain

IT wasn't long after I arrived in Orlando that an opportunity to work on music presented itself. A coworker knew of someone who had a home studio and brought me over to meet him. My first producer was positive, creative, hard working, yet laid back at the same time. We started with the idea of a demo but, after recording three songs, decided to move ahead with a full album called *Transcending*. I would buy beats created by different producers on his record label, one at a time, that we thought would frame the lyrics in my poems nicely. I reworked the structure of them and repeated certain lines so they sounded more like songs over a trip hop beat. Although a couple tracks were cut from the final mix and some instrumental tracks were added, I still ended up with a solo album that flowed smoothly from start to finish. I decided to shoot the cover, which got a lot of attention locally and people started asking why I didn't model professionally.

This is a shot of the dress I wore to the national pageant.

This was taken backstage at an awards show in which I was performing.

My high school friends talked me into running track,
but during down time you could see me reading.
This photo appeared in the local newspaper and
foreshadowed things to come, as I eventually followed
my dream to become a writing professor.

Finally on my own,
it was nice to walk
with my friends
without hiding a
secret life that was
filled with torment.

I was eager to showcase my lyrics,
but shooting the cover of my first album
soon led to my modeling career.

CHAPTER THREE

BLUE RIDGE BLUES

Dropped from the Mountaintop

I didn't have much time to promote the album be cause my childhood sweetheart would cross my path again when I was nineteen. After he had signed a record deal in Nashville just before my junior year, I had given him an ultimatum to commit to our relationship. He didn't call or write much and, after four and a half years, I was beginning to feel forgotten as he traveled around the country opening up for famous country artists.

I wanted to go to the prom like my other friends in high school and just have a normal life, as I wasn't get-ting love or affection from a family at home. He told me that we were teenagers and didn't know what love is, proceeding to try and convince me not to date other guys while avoiding the topic at hand. I had given up and was convinced he would forget about me until my mom, always pulling strings behind the scenes, orchestrated another meeting with myself and his brothers in Lake City, Florida.

I met up with him, having slim to no expectations, checking into my own hotel room next to the one his brothers had rented. At one point, he came into my room and sat on my bed, playing me a song. It was a song he had written about me and I struggled to hold myself together, not letting the familiar feelings flood back over me. Would he just pull me back into the same waiting game if I devoted myself to him again?

My heart won out just months later, after he sent me a message to call him. When I did, he begged me to attend his cousin's wedding in Virginia. I protested that I hadn't been invited and wasn't sure if they even wanted to see me (as I had stopped my summer visits to see his family after our breakup). "But *I'll* be there. You can see *me*," he said softly with a vulnerability in his voice that I hadn't seen since the whirlwind of his music career had turned him cocky and aloof.

I agreed and was welcomed back with open arms into his extended family. His mother then "prophesied" that it was God's will for me to be there and my talents would have been used for "the world" if not . . . that

God had saved me from being "ensnared in a trap." The words were foreboding and dramatic, but although I didn't think there was anything wrong with me pursuing a music career of my own, I couldn't resist the feeling of being finally accepted by a family unit (with the promise of creating a family of my own with the love of my life). I packed up all my things, letting my cell phone and email account go (since I wouldn't be working there). I then went along with his mother's plan for me to move in to the church owned by his family, attending a Bible school on the grounds.

My dreams of a white picket fence started to fade, however, as my first semester wore on. Though he moved his things back to his parents' house in the tiny mountain town where he grew up, my love only came home once a month to check on me and see how things were going. He still wasn't calling or writing in between visits, but I spent every day with his aunts, uncles, and cousins. I even had phone conversations with his brothers on the one telephone that hung on the wall in the basement of the church (our "dorm"). I felt isolated from my old life in Florida, growing more and more attached to his family members, but desperately missing him.

The Making of a Perfect Christian Wife

THE environment at seminary was strict with a set schedule for prayer, worship, and studying. The dress code was centered around the concepts of modesty and purity. Being from one of the hottest states in the country where it never snowed, most of my wardrobe was thrown out in a large black, garbage bag—deemed inappropriate or revealing. I adapted, but started seeing lots of red flags. Girls were encouraged to cut off relationships with boyfriends back home once they were in school there. Romantic relationships were discouraged the first year and had to be approved by "leadership" the second year. Since I was halfway through the first year when I was enrolled in the "college," we would only have to wait six months to be "approved." The elders consisted of my sweetheart's family members and father, so I wasn't too concerned (although his father didn't seem keen on any of his sons getting married and leaving the family business/ministry).

One day, my secret pain seemed to come to an unbearable point when the choir director screamed at us, "It's not about you, it's about God!" Apparently, I was projecting my voice and it seemed too showy for her taste, as she was glaring right at me when she yelled. Dejected, I ran to my room after practice and looked in the mirror. Seeing my hair growing out again (after cutting it to my shoulders senior year, much to my then ex's dismay), the skirt down to my ankles, and the light of creativity drained from my eyes, I realized I was losing my individuality.

"I don't know who I am if I'm not a singer," I thought to myself. Soon after, I was cut from a solo I was supposed to sing at the graduation ceremony for the second year class with a talented pianist from my first year group. Even the dean of students (who I had called "uncle" since I joined the family at age ten) congratulated me after delivering a sermon I had worked hard on, but then warned not to let it "go to my head."

They looked at women as created for a "helpmate" to men, not allowed to further their education in any specific field (unless working for a company owned by a church elder) or even have jobs outside the compound of adjoining farms. I had to get permission to work at a Christian music store where I was paid in CDs to replace the secular music I was ordered to throw out upon arrival to the church. I remember writing in my diary about my feelings and seeing the words really made it clear that I had to leave.

When my "boyfriend" didn't come home to see me two months in a row, that was all the proof I needed that I had been sold a bill of goods and he had no intention of following through with his promises of building us a house and starting a family. I drove to Florida under the guise of visiting once school let out for the summer, but instead picked up my best friend and brought her back to the compound with me. Unnerved by the rituals she witnessed, she commented that it seemed "like a cult." She helped me pack all my things in my car in the middle of the night before escaping after church the next day. Although the dorm mother tried to block our exit, there was not much she could do, as they did not know my best friend's family and could not manipulate to keep an "outsider" there. We drove back to Florida and I cut all ties with my mother, the church, and my (again) ex's family.

CHAPTER FOUR

RACING DOWN THE RUNWAY

I Was Already "There" and Didn't Know It

Back in Florida, I finally listened to the many people who had suggested I take up modeling professionally. After sending out submission after submission, I got my first agent. Eventually I worked for twenty nonexclusive agents and fifteen marketing companies, located in five different states. I had pretty much become a local celebrity in Orlando while constantly traveling to Tampa and Miami Beach for gigs. I was on call 24/7 and worked every day. I didn't take a vacation for four years and the strain started to become obvious to me after I booked an appearance on an international television show.

Driving back across the bridge from an audition in South Beach, I remembered a passage from a book I had read, written by a popular pastor. It talked about how some people are already "there," but they don't even know it. I realized suddenly that I was pushing myself much too hard. When you work as an independent contractor, you are essentially unemployed after each gig wraps. I was always worried about where my next paycheck was coming from or how I could push up to the next level—so much so that I never stopped to celebrate wins. I was racking up the accolades, building status in the industry, but I still felt insecure and unfulfilled. I told myself right then, "You are going to be proud of yourself for at least *two* days." Nevertheless, the very next day, I was back to beating myself up again.

Knowing When to Step Offstage

AFTER that epiphany in Miami, I decided to walk away from modeling and pursue a college degree. Having recently finished recording my second album (the studio time for which I had to squeeze in between my statewide commutes for auditions, runway shows, and television spots), I realized that many of the musicians around me were still struggling to make it. They didn't have a backup plan. I chose a degree that would still provide a creative outlet, though, as a degree in writing would sharpen my songwriting and poetry skills.

Thinking back on how hard I had worked for my scholarship in high school, I realized my singing had been the focus a lot more than my writing since I loved the feeling of being onstage. I got a little bit of that on the runway, but it didn't quite match the visceral sensation of using your voice at the same time. Writing had always been my second passion, so I once again put music on the back burner and turned my attention to my studies.

A Familiar Pattern

AT about twenty-two years old, a couple of years before I quit modeling, I had taken a trip to Los Angeles to see if I could sign with one of the top agencies in the industry. I fell in love with it right away and took another trip there the summer after my junior year in college. I was in L.A. for five days and there seemed to be a magic in the air. I hung out with a musician that I had met on spring break back when I was modeling in Florida. He introduced me to his bandmates and by the end of the trip, we had talked about doing a side project in the future.

Though looking back, it may have seemed like just a late night idea that sounded good in the moment, his best friend and I took it more seriously and had many discussions about the direction that project could take. These guys were very talented, I believed in their band, and I was excited at the possibility of being professionally involved with them in any way. Seven months after meeting them, I bought an SUV, packed it up with all my belongings, and drove across the country to start a new chapter in California.

Things didn't turn out quite like I had planned. The band was really busy with their latest project and didn't have time to work with me. I understood since scheduling issues arose quite often in the music industry. I supported them as best I could while finishing up my bachelors degree, often carpooling with their instruments to shows or taking video and photos of their performances. As the months went on, though, we grew apart. They were getting girlfriends and I was getting in the way.

I kept writing the songs I had wanted to show them and instead kept them for a potential pop/rock album. I met a producer who was a touring bassist for an Irish punk band at the time, so my solo project idea took a back seat to his busy schedule. I still wasn't phased, but decided to write down a list of every music contact I knew and send them demos. I vowed to make it happen in my own strength once again, just like I did when

I modeled . . . until one day, I sat back and took a hard look at my new life.

I was living in the Hollywood Hills, in a townhouse with a charming courtyard shared by my neighbors on Beachwood Drive. It was so beautiful, with hardwood floors, a fireplace, and a black wrought iron staircase to my room which had a view of picturesque, green trees. I felt like on the outside, my life looked perfect, but it was so empty. I was lonely, working two jobs, and had to remind myself to get outside at least once a week. Even when I did, it was hard to find people to walk with on my journey. The city moved at a fast pace and my friends had started feeling more like acquaintances.

Knowing there had to be more that I was missing, I went back to church and rededicated my life to God. I wanted to keep Him first in my life and trust that if my music was meant to happen, it would happen in His timing. Throughout my twenties, I had kept my career first, justifying that I had to take care of myself. Traumatized by being a teenage runaway, I still struggled to feel safe and secure. Remembering how I got burned out on modeling, I didn't want my workaholic tendencies to ruin my passion for music.

Here's me with my travel suitcase packed.
I was always on call when I was a runway model.

This was me after
an audition in South
Beach, on the rare
occasion I got a hotel
and met up with
friends instead of
driving all the way
back to Orlando
the same day.

This was me
modeling
evening gowns
at a high-end
shopping mall.

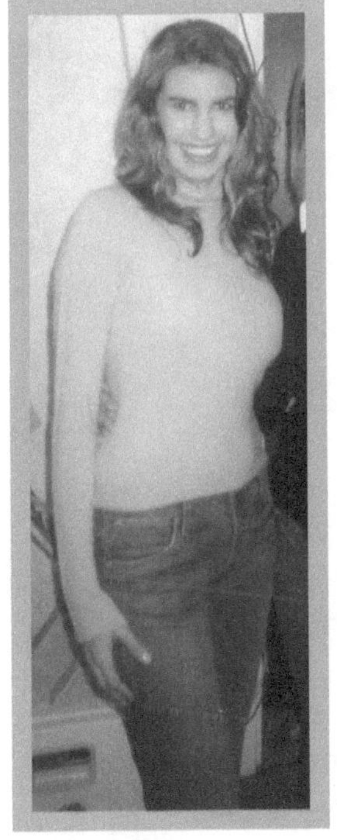

I modeled jeans for curvy
women on live tv for a
national morning show.

This was the photo on the front of my last comp card as a model. It was also available as a full size poster, which hung at my album release party for *Intrinsically*.

When I was 23, I flew to Los Angeles to look for a new modeling agent and fell in love with the city—especially Malibu.

CHAPTER FIVE

HOW A PASTOR HELPED ME "COPE"

Hanging Up My Cap and Gown

TWENTY-EIGHT was a pivotal year for me. About a month after I graduated from college, the housing crisis of 2008 took place and work started to be more scarce as the country moved towards a recession. Feeling like I had given Los Angeles a year and a fighting chance, I headed back to Orlando to attend graduate school (which I hoped could help me compete in an increasingly tough job market). I kept God first and prayed before major decisions, though, often volunteering at a local church.

I loved grad school and narrowed my track to music, focusing on concert promotion. I hoped to get a job with a live music venue or tour. In the back of my mind, I still believed that once I achieved a certain level of success, my family would accept me. My mother had continued to hurt me from a distance, refusing an offer to go to counseling, then turning family members against me during my twenties (although my adoptive grandmother stayed a constant in my life through the ups and downs).

My graduation day arrived, but there had been no reconciliation with my extended family. I was crushed when I had to attend the ceremony without my new boyfriend, who did not want to ask off work at his new job. He didn't understand why the day meant so much to me, since he didn't walk with his own class. I guess as a little girl, when attending family events, I always thought that's what my own life would look like when I grew up. Instead, I had been struggling through the years, hoping that my friends would invite me to their family holiday gatherings. Many of my own milestones and victories went unacknowledged.

Heartbroken, I couldn't help but think, "I did all this for nothing. My boyfriend and I drifted apart. I had hoped to have a child by my late twenties, so this made things even harder. A diary entry from that time period captured some of my pain:

The walls feel like they're closing in on me. There's pain in my head and pressure in my chest. It's debilitating. Here I am again. No place to go. Painted into a corner. The lifestyle I used to love turned from a dreamlike escape into a nightmare. . . .

As soon as night falls, I am alone. There is nothing but the sound of the mini-fridge in my studio apartment and trains in the distance. Now I cannot busy myself with running odd errands and finishing my schoolwork at the library. I'll have to face the facts. There's no one to go home to. Diplomas and ribbons lie packed up in boxes, since there's no one to show them to—no reason to put them on display.

Rededicating My Life to Religion

I remember a local pastor had a conversation with me at our church in Winter Park. Not entirely sure what returning to a Christian lifestyle should look like (after being raised in such a legalistic "church"), I had continued to strive to be the perfect Christian. I kept at arms length for fear church people would hurt me again, but joined lots of groups to try and work on my faith. One Sunday, after confessing yet another mistake and asking if he thought God still had grace for me, my pastor encouraged me. "Jennifer," he said, "I see you come to church week after week because you truly believe that God can transform your life. . . . It's not what you do.

It's *who you are.*" Though I had walked away from the entertainment industry for a season and rededicated my life to God, my behaviors seemed set on spin cycle.

Performance Mentality

THE pattern that kept reappearing in my life was performance mentality. The first time I heard the term, it made so much sense. It was at church, in regards to "faith versus works." A lady who I looked up to explained to me that God's love for us is unconditional, that Jesus finished the work of forgiveness on the cross. This was in direct conflict with the way I was raised. After all, my church "family" had turned their backs on me when I wouldn't continue my performance to look, dress, and act like them. When I chose to educate myself and pursue a career, my ex's mother had told me she would have to do "tough love" on me, then they all turned their backs on me. It seemed it didn't matter how hard I worked in school, in the entertainment industry, or in church . . . the common thread was that I still felt unaccepted, unwanted, and unloved.

I had stars in my eyes after getting my writing degree,
looking forward to the future.

In contrast to my undergrad ceremony,
I had been crying all morning so there are
dark circles under my eyes here.

CHAPTER SIX

PICKING UP THE PIECES

A Different Kind of Praise

AT job interviews, employers often ask you to describe yourself using a few words. Some of my go-to's in the past have been "friendly," "outgoing," "dependable," or "hardworking." Now that I look back on it, the writing had always been on the wall. I was a workaholic and a people pleaser. I thought these qualities made me likable and worth taking a chance on. Instead, those tendencies eventually wreaked havoc on my health, causing unhealthy stress.

They also took a toll on my personal life. As if interviewing for a job, I would present myself on a first date with my best foot forward. However, all I got was a string of abusive, dishonest, selfish boyfriends who reinforced my fear that I would always be abandoned (just like my father had abandoned me). I struggled to find my value and worth outside of my external accomplishments, but the more I achieved, the more it eluded me. Soon I found myself single in my thirties with a suitcase full of emotional baggage from the years of pain, heartbreak, and disappointment.

Self-Care Isn't Selfish; It's Self-Esteem

ASIDE from all the classes and church meetings, one of the best things I did that year was attending a self help group for codependency. In Los Angeles, one of the first things I noticed was how lost I felt without the group of friends I had built in Orlando—a sort of second family (since mine was absent). Although it was an exciting adventure, I had trouble enjoying it because I was often alone.

Back home, I faced this issue once again after my new boyfriend emotionally abandoned me. I found this support group helpful so that I didn't stay in an unhealthy relationship where my needs were being ignored. I slowly learned how to meet my own needs. I learned about boundaries—how to set them and enforce them.

I have finished college now, but still struggle to find solid, steady employment in a field that is quickly turning into a gig economy (higher education). I have had to take temporary adjunct instructor assignments and work various odd jobs to get by. This has caused me a lot of stress, so I recently had to prioritize my health. I have learned to set limits and say "no" to certain opportunities that don't align with my life goals. This was something I struggled with back when I was a runway model. I would snatch up every job offer I could find. I even had to turn down a gig on a soap opera once because I was sick and had a math test the next day (which I had to study for). Now I understand the importance of listening to your body.

CHAPTER SEVEN

FROM FRAGILE FLOWER TO POWERFUL PRINCESS

Princess in a Tower

LIKE most little girls, I have always loved stories about fairy tale princesses. One day in church, I had a vision of a princess walking up a winding staircase inside a castle tower. As she approached a door, I noticed that she was holding a set of keys. Inside the bedroom was a girl that looked just like her, but she was lying down on a bed—depressed and crying. I heard God say to me that a vision of my identity would help unlock me from the prison of depression. For so long, I have been sad about not having a family and have been trying in vain to fill that void.

Several years after I had that vision, I had the chance to attend a conference on identity where a Christian inner healing minister was speaking. She has always been a role model to me since I met her in Nashville on one of my work trips. I knew that this was an important step in my healing.

Promises, promises . . . or His Promises

I N the Bible, King David warns, "Do not put your trust in princes, in human beings, who cannot save" (Psalms 146:3, NIV). I have had a tendency to be that girl. Lacking a father's love, I sought affection and protection from men. Reading self-help books and attending church has helped me to hold on to my hope, but I made so many mistakes along the way, wanting so desperately to be loved.

I had another vision while I was attending what's called a "soaking" group (where you listen to music and just soak up God's presence). A musician friend had invited me and I was skeptical at first, but the picture I saw in my mind during the group really changed my outlook on my circumstances. In this vision, there was a girl in a long dress lying on the side of the road, holding her stomach. I realized that it was me around the age of twenty. Then, guy after guy came by and (to my horror) kicked the girl in the stomach. There was blood all over the ground.

God whispered, "When I look at you, that's how I see you." It was the first time I truly realized that God saw my heart and had compassion for me. My childhood sweetheart had disagreed on how many children we wanted to have. I wasn't sure if we could afford five, since I was just a waitress and he was bankrupt after his record deal. I asserted that we could have one, *maybe* two, but the dream of at least having a son with him was very much alive in my mind and heart. The girl lying on the ground, abandoned, had lost her baby—just like I lost my dream of a child.

And I couldn't seem to get back up. . . .

God's Country

THROUGHOUT the turmoils and trials in my life, Mamaw was always there for me. When I talked to her about my travels, she preferred Nashville out of all the places I'd visited and lived. Being from Alabama herself, she said, "Tennessee is so beautiful. It's *God's* country." That stood out in my mind and, a few months after I made a permanent move there, she went to Heaven. I remember her saying towards the end of her life here on Earth, "I want to see you *happy*."

After a hospital scare eight years earlier, she felt she was on borrowed time, but I always believed deep down that she stayed partly because of me (as I wasn't in the safest of situations during my time in L.A.). She was content with me being in Tennessee and that brings me peace. I have a good life here, filled with long drives in the country and deep talks with the spiritual mothers God has been sending me along the way in her absence.

CHAPTER EIGHT

FROM BRIGHT LIGHTS TO BEACON OF HOPE

Kind of Like the Life I've Always Dreamed Of

My most recent work of art is an EP that I released this year, titled *Kind of Like the Life I've Always Dreamed Of.* I call it "inspirational pop" and it includes five new, original songs which I have been performing at writers' nights in Nashville. One of the most exciting things about living here is that I have been blessed to meet some of my role models in the industry, including my favorite actress and a supermodel that I looked up to when I was younger. I've even crossed paths with some friends from Orlando. Though we might be in different places (many have married and are raising children), they continue to inspire me and I cherish the memories of our adolescence in the pop music scene of the 90's.

My new direction is based on how I envision God working through my experiences. In fact, the title track of my EP says it best:

Now He's putting back together all the pieces of my life and I know everything happens for a reason. Through it all, He's painting me a picture of His love. It looks kind of like the life I've always dreamed of.

The lyrics tell the story of a girl who, after putting her faith in God and trusting Him to guide her life, wakes up one day to look around at all her blessings. She realizes that He has been painting a masterpiece all along, though she didn't always understand what He was up to. This is the vision I had for the EP and as I've walked through the steps of writing, recording, releasing, and promoting it, the lyrics have become somewhat of a self-fulfilling prophecy. That's the great thing about art, especially the kind that is positive and uplifting—the more you focus on it, the more inspiration it creates.

Jewels in His Crown

RECENTLY, I have felt called to apply what I've learned on my journey to help other entertainers. I especially feel drawn to help women in the industry, as they face so many unique pressures, including body image issues and gender inequality within the workforce. They are often paid less than men, which is coming more to the forefront of public awareness as of late. If you listen to the lyrics of many mainstream musicians, you can hear the struggles they go through coming across in their art—including feelings of never being good enough or thin enough. They even share thoughts of loneliness, as their career pulls them away from relationships when they travel.

Although I've had a chance to do so during my five years as an adjunct professor, I would also like to help these artists through coaching. I created Jewels in His Crown Coaching to do just that, inspired by a Bible verse. It reads, "The Lord their God will save his people on that day as a shepherd saves his flock. They will sparkle in His land like jewels in a crown" (Zechariah 9:16, NIV).

I was certified through a church in California and look forward to this new endeavor. I continue to work on my own art, so that I can share and express my gifts. I know that God is still moving in my life in new ways every day that I wake up, lining up things to work out for my good.

My hope is that everyone reading this can encounter the God who created you and loves you for *you*. If you grew up in a religion based on fear, I pray that you encounter His amazing grace. If you are alone, I pray that He surrounds you with safe people and community. If you are hurting, I pray that He heals your heart and sets you free. He has a plan and a purpose for your existence.

CONCLUSION

IMAGE, persona, fashion, status, and reputation are things that so many Americans worry about. Like shifting sand, the trends change and popularity wanes. In the Bible, King Solomon asks, "What do people gain from all their labors at which they toll under the sun?" (Ecclesiastes 1:3, NIV). Money and fame can be taken away, yet so many people place their self value and worth on the external things we can obtain to define us.

This is just one story, one perspective on an issue that is widespread throughout the globe and has been present throughout history. In light of eternity, it's who we are and not what we do that will leave a lasting impression on the lives of those around us. In my work, I encounter many teenagers and young adults who are managing their dreams, goals, and aspirations on their own for the first time. It can be overwhelming to try and fit in while also being your own unique individual (who may be balancing an increasing set of responsibilities).

Many college students that I have taught are stressed, insecure, and frustrated. Unaware of the damage this can cause, they oftentimes don't seek treatment until they get physically sick or their grades are affected. If you are reading this book and this resounds with you, know that there are many resources to help you.

Most colleges offer counseling, as do churches and local nonprofit organizations. You may be able to ask for financial assistance (i.e., a sliding scale for payment, based on your income) with the costs. Self help books are great, but there's also no shame in seeking professional help. Group therapy and support groups can help you realize that you're not alone in your struggle.

Individual therapy can help you get to the root of past traumas that can be causing you present hurt, keeping you from reaching your full potential. Once you are ready to move forward, a life coach can help you identify other obstacles that are getting in your way and set an action plan to help you realize your dreams.

RESOURCES

Counseling

Porters Call
(615) 591-6622
www.porterscall.com
sidnye@porterscall.com

Emergency Financial Assistance

MusiCares
West Region — (310)392-3777
South Region — (615)327-0050
East Region — (212) 245-7840
addiction recovery programs also available

Musicians Foundation

(212) 239-9137
www.musiciansfoundation.org

Health Care Services

Music Health Alliance
(615) 200-6896
www.musichealthalliance.com
info@musichealthalliance.com

National Domestic Violence Hotline

(800) 799-7233
www.thehotline.org

Victim Advocacy

G.R.A.C.E.
(Godly Response to Abuse in
the Christian Environment)
info@netgrace.org
www.netgrace.org

Dr. Jennifer "Kaylene" Carter began working in the entertainment industry at the age of thirteen, alongside many up-and-coming stars in Orlando's pop music scene. As a teenager, she transitioned from acting to singing, recording her first solo album (which she wrote and coproduced) during her senior year of high school. She also worked as a dancer and a runway model, making several appearances on both national and international television. A second solo album followed, which showcased her artistic versatility and style.

Kaylene's career led her to creative projects in Los Angeles, Nashville, and New York City. Taking her love of lyric to the next level, she pursued advanced degrees in Creative Writing and Entertainment Business. Driven by her passion for poetry and songwriting, she is now working as a professor and life coach for entertainers.